Tudor England

While every precaution has been taken in the preparation of this book, the publisher assumes no responsibility for errors or omissions, or for damages resulting from the use of the information contained herein.

TUDOR ENGLAND

First edition. May 11, 2024.

Copyright © 2024 History Nerds.

ISBN: 979-8227272713

Written by History Nerds.

Also by History Nerds

Ancient Empires
The Ottoman Empire
Rome: The Rise and Fall
The Mongol Empire
The Assyrian Empire
Ancient Egypt

Celtic Heroes and Legends
Celtic History
William Butler Yeats: Nobel Prize Winning Poet
Robert the Bruce
Scáthach
Finn McCool
William Wallace: Scotland's Great Freedom Fighter

Frauen des Krieges
Boudica: Königin der Icener
Jeanne d'Arc

Irena Sendler

Great Wars of the World
World War 1
World War 2
The Napoleonic Wars: One Shot at Glory
The Serbian Revolution: 1804-1835
Peace Won by the Saber: The Crimean War, 1853-1856
The American Civil War

Pirate Chronicles
Grace O'Malley: The Pirate Queen of Ireland
Blackbeard
William Kidd
Ching Shih
Anne Bonny

The History of England
Roman Britain
Medieval England
The Wars of the Roses
Tudor England

The History of the Vikings

Vikings
Longships on Restless Seas

Women of War
Boudica: Queen of the Iceni
Joan of Arc
Irena Sendler
Virginia Hall
Queen Amanirenas
Women of War Omnibus: Books 1-5

World History
The History of the United Kingdom
The History of Ireland
The History of America
The History of Scotland
The History of Wales
The History of India

Standalone
Grace O'Malley: Die Piratenkönigin von Irland

Table of Contents

Introduction

The Emergence of the Tudors: A Pivotal Epoch in England's Storied Past

In the annals of English history, few dynasties have left an indelible mark as profound as the Tudors. Their reign, spanning over a century from 1485 to 1603, witnessed the transformation of a once-fragmented nation into a burgeoning empire, a shift that would reverberate across the globe for centuries to come.

The ascension of Henry VII to the throne, following the culmination of the War of the Roses at the Battle of Bosworth Field, heralded the dawn of a new era—one that would reshape the very fabric of English society, governance, and religious identity.

The Tudor epoch, often regarded as a renaissance for England, was a period of immense complexity and change. It saw the consolidation of royal authority, the emergence of a centralized state apparatus, and the establishment of England as a formidable force on the European stage. Yet, amidst these monumental shifts, the Tudors also navigated an intricate web of internal dynamics, grappling with religious upheaval, economic reforms, and cultural flourishing, all of which left an indelible imprint on the nation's trajectory.

This book delves into the multifaceted legacy of the Tudor monarchs, examining their impact across a vast tapestry of domains. From the calculated maneuverings of Henry VII to secure the throne and solidify his dynasty's grip on power, to the tumultuous reign of Henry VIII and his seismic break with the Roman Catholic Church, the Tudors' relentless pursuit of control and autonomy reshaped England's religious landscape irrevocably.

The book also explores the profound economic and legal reforms instituted under the Tudors, which laid the groundwork for England's emergence as a commercial powerhouse and set the stage for the expansion of its global influence.

Beyond the realms of politics and governance, the Tudor era witnessed a remarkable cultural renaissance, with the flourishing of art, literature, and intellectual discourse. From the poetic genius of William Shakespeare to the pioneering explorations of Walter Raleigh, the Tudors fostered an environment that nurtured creativity and encouraged the pursuit of knowledge. This rich cultural legacy serves as a testament to the vibrant intellectual climate that permeated England during this transformative period.

The book's narrative arc spans the reigns of the five Tudor monarchs—Henry VII, Henry VIII, Edward VI, Mary I, and Elizabeth I—each chapter offering an in-depth exploration of their respective legacies and contributions to the shaping of modern England. From Henry VII's deft political maneuverings and the establishment of the Tudor dynasty, to the tumultuous religious upheavals and marital intrigues of Henry VIII, the book navigates the intricate tapestry of Tudor history with nuanced insights and meticulous attention to detail.

Edward VI's short but impactful reign, marked by the solidification of the Protestant Reformation in England, paves the way for the subsequent Catholic revival under Mary I, whose efforts to restore the Catholic faith were met with fierce resistance and ultimately overshadowed by the glory of her successor, Elizabeth I. The book culminates with Elizabeth's remarkable reign, characterized by a period of unparalleled cultural and intellectual flourishing, the expansion of England's global reach, and the consolidation of the nation's Protestant identity.

The Tudor era, with its rich tapestry of political intrigue, religious turmoil, and cultural Renaissance, stands as a pivotal chapter in England's storied history. By exploring the lives, legacies, and profound impact of the Tudor monarchs, this book offers readers a comprehensive and nuanced understanding of an era that continues to shape the fabric of modern English society and governance. Through meticulous research and insightful analysis, the narrative unveils the complexities and enduring influence of a dynasty that forever altered the trajectory of a nation, leaving an indelible imprint on the world beyond England's shores.

Henry VII - The Dawn of the Tudor Era

Reign 1485-1509

The Prelude to Power

How did one decisive battle reshape the course of English history and pave the way for a dynasty that would transform the nation?

At the dawn of the 15th century, England found itself embroiled in a prolonged and bitter conflict known as the War of the Roses. This internecine struggle between the Houses of Lancaster and York for control of the English throne had plunged the nation into a state of chaos and instability. Years of strife and bloodshed had taken a heavy toll, with the once-prosperous realm teetering on the brink of disarray.

The question of succession to the English throne was not merely a matter of royal lineage; it carried profound implications for the nation's future trajectory. The War of the Roses had exposed the fragility of the existing political order and highlighted the need for a decisive shift in leadership that could restore stability and unity. This pivotal moment in history begged for a resolution that would bring an end to the turmoil and usher in a new era of governance and prosperity.

The problem at hand was a complex web of competing claims to the throne, fueled by deep-seated rivalries and the ambitions of powerful noble houses. The House of Lancaster, represented by Henry VI, had held the throne for decades, but their grip on power had been weakened by the king's mental instability and the growing influence of the House of York, led by the formidable Richard Plantagenet. As the conflict escalated, the kingdom found itself divided, with loyalties splintered and the prospect of a lasting peace seeming increasingly elusive.

Conventional approaches to resolving such conflicts often involved protracted negotiations, fragile alliances, or outright capitulation by one side. However, these methods had proven ineffective in the face of the deep-rooted animosity between the warring factions. The kingdom needed a decisive, transformative solution – one that would not only end the conflict but also lay the foundation for a new era of stability and prosperity.

The Battle of Bosworth Field, fought on August 22, 1485, marked a turning point in this turbulent chapter of English history. It was here that Henry Tudor, a relatively obscure claimant to the throne, emerged victorious against the formidable forces of Richard III, the last Yorkist king. Henry's triumph, against seemingly insurmountable odds, ushered in a new era – the Tudor dynasty.

Henry Tudor's victory at Bosworth Field was not merely a military triumph; it was a strategic masterstroke that showcased his political acumen and ability to forge strategic alliances. By aligning himself with powerful allies, including the influential Stanley family and the French monarch, Henry demonstrated a keen understanding of the intricate power dynamics at play. His victory was not simply a matter of might but a calculated and well-executed campaign that capitalized on the weaknesses of his opponents and the shifting tides of popular sentiment.

Critics and skeptics might argue that Henry's claim to the throne was tenuous at best, given the long-standing rivalry between the Houses of Lancaster and York. However, Henry's masterful maneuvering and ability to rally support from diverse factions underscored his political savvy and the recognition that a decisive break from the past was necessary to restore stability and order to the realm.

To solidify his position and establish the foundations of the Tudor dynasty, Henry VII took decisive action upon assuming the throne. He moved swiftly to neutralize potential threats, forging strategic marriages and alliances to consolidate his power base. Additionally, he implemented far-reaching reforms to strengthen the monarchy's authority, centralize governance, and foster economic growth. By addressing the root causes of instability and embracing a forward-looking vision, Henry paved the way for a transformative era that would redefine England's place on the world stage.

If you wish to delve deeper into the intricacies of this pivotal moment in history and understand how the Battle of Bosworth Field reshaped the destiny of a nation, I invite you to explore our book on The Wars of the Roses. We will however cover some details on the war as we look into the reign of Henry VII. Through a detailed analysis of the political machinations, strategic alliances, and visionary reforms of Henry VII, you will gain a deeper appreciation for the enduring legacy of the Tudor dynasty and the profound impact it had on shaping the England we know today.

Consolidating the Crown

After a decisive victory at the Battle of Bosworth Field in 1485, Henry immediately set to work consolidating his power and establishing the Tudor dynasty. His goal, to unite a fractured nation and secure his position as the undisputed monarch, laying the foundation for a new era in English history.

The primary challenge Henry VII faced was uniting a nation torn apart by years of conflict between the Houses of Lancaster and York during the War of the Roses. He needed to establish his legitimacy as the rightful monarch, quell potential uprisings from rival factions, and heal the deep divisions that had plagued the realm. To that end, Henry VII married Elizabeth of York, solidifying his claim to the throne by uniting the Houses of Lancaster and York. This symbolic union helped reconcile opposing factions and garnered support from Yorkist supporters. Henry officially established the Tudor dynasty, marking a clean break from the past and signaling a new era of governance and stability. He also rewarded loyal supporters with titles, lands, and positions of influence, while neutralizing potential threats through strategic appointments, exiles, and executions. Also implemented were reforms to centralize power and authority in the monarchy, including the formation of a professional bureaucracy and the establishment of the Court of Star. Recognizing the importance of a strong economy, Henry VII introduced measures to promote trade, stabilize currency, and increase royal revenues, laying the foundation for future prosperity.

Henry VII successfully united the warring factions, ending the decades-long conflict of the War of the Roses and ushering in a period of relative peace and stability. Through his marriage to Elizabeth of York and the birth of their son, Henry VIII, Henry VII established a clear line of succession for the Tudor dynasty. The reforms implemented by Henry VII consolidated the power of the monarchy, laying the groundwork for the absolute rule of his successors. The economic policies and initiatives introduced by Henry VII helped revive trade, stabilize finances, and set the stage for England's future prosperity.

Henry VII's strategic maneuvers and compromises, while effective, could be seen as opportunistic and calculated, prioritizing political expediency over ideological principles. Critics argued that his harsh treatment of potential rivals and consolidation of power laid the foundations for the later excesses of the Tudor monarchs and contributed to the erosion of traditional checks and balances. Alternatively, Henry VII's actions could be viewed as pragmatic and necessary steps to unite a fractured nation and prevent further conflict, paving the way for a golden age of English history.

While Henry VII's actions were often driven by political expediency, his ability to navigate complex challenges and forge strategic alliances ultimately proved instrumental in uniting a fractured nation and ushering in a new era of stability and prosperity. The legacy of the Tudor dynasty would forever shape the course of English history, serving as a testament to the enduring impact of decisive leadership and visionary governance.

Economic Reforms: Rebuilding a Realm

The War of the Roses had not only decimated the nobility and claimed countless lives but also left the kingdom in a state of disrepair, with trade disrupted, public coffers drained, and a weakened currency undermining economic stability. Recognizing the pivotal role of a robust economy in cementing his newfound power, the prudent king took decisive steps to revive England's financial fortunes, implementing a series of reforms that would shape the nation's trajectory for generations to come.

The War of the Roses had taken a devastating toll on England's economy. Years of conflict had disrupted trade routes, deterring merchants from conducting business and leaving the kingdom's coffers depleted. The debasement of coinage to fund the war efforts had eroded public confidence in the currency, leading to rampant inflation and economic uncertainty. Moreover, the feuding noble houses had amassed considerable wealth and power, posing a potential threat to the monarch's authority and undermining attempts at centralized governance. Without a stable economic foundation, Henry VII's reign would remain vulnerable to challenges from disgruntled factions, jeopardizing the hard-won peace and stability he sought to establish.

Failure to address the economic upheaval could have dire consequences for the fledgling Tudor dynasty. A weakened currency and depleted treasury would hinder the crown's ability to fund essential functions, such as maintaining a standing army or financing diplomatic endeavors. Unchecked inflation and economic instability could fuel public discontent, providing fertile ground for rival claimants to the throne to galvanize support and challenge Henry VII's legitimacy. Furthermore, the concentration of wealth and power in the hands of the nobility could embolden their ambitions, potentially leading to further conflict and undermining the monarch's authority. Without decisive action, the kingdom risked sliding back into chaos, squandering the opportunity to heal the deep wounds of the past and build a prosperous future.

Recognizing the inextricable link between economic stability and political power, Henry VII embarked on a series of far-reaching economic reforms aimed at reviving England's financial fortunes and consolidating his authority. His strategy was multifaceted, addressing issues of taxation, trade, and currency regulation, demonstrating a keen understanding of the intricate relationship between economic policy and statecraft.

One of the first steps taken by Henry VII was to overhaul the kingdom's taxation system. He sought to centralize the collection and administration of taxes, reducing the reliance on the feudal system and the often-capricious whims of local lords. By establishing a more efficient and equitable system of taxation, the crown could generate a steady stream of revenue to fund its operations and initiatives.

Notably, Henry VII introduced new forms of taxation, such as the infamous "Morton's Fork," named after his Chancellor, John Morton. This ingenious scheme targeted both the wealthy and the poor, levying taxes based on their perceived ability to pay. Those who lived lavishly were deemed wealthy enough to contribute substantial sums, while those with modest lifestyles were presumed to have hidden away considerable savings and were likewise taxed. This approach, while controversial, allowed the king to tap into previously untapped sources of revenue, replenishing the royal coffers and funding his ambitious plans.

Recognizing the importance of a thriving mercantile sector, Henry VII implemented policies to promote trade and commerce. He negotiated favorable treaties with other nations, opening new markets for English goods and securing advantageous terms for English merchants. Additionally, he invested in the construction and maintenance of roads, bridges, and ports, facilitating the movement of goods and reducing the costs associated with transportation.

To further incentivize trade, the king granted charters to trading companies, granting them monopolies in specific regions or commodities. This not only encouraged investment and entrepreneurship but also allowed the crown to regulate and tax these lucrative ventures, generating additional revenue while fostering economic growth.

Addressing the issue of a debased and unstable currency was a crucial component of Henry VII's economic strategy. He took steps to restore confidence in the English coinage, issuing new, high-quality coins with a standardized weight and purity. This move not only stabilized the currency but also signaled the king's commitment to sound financial practices, reassuring merchants and investors alike.

Henry VII's economic reforms yielded tangible and far-reaching results, solidifying his reign and laying the foundation for England's future prosperity. By stabilizing the currency and restoring confidence in the kingdom's financial system, he facilitated a resurgence in trade and commerce. Merchants and investors, reassured by the government's commitment to sound economic policies, were more willing to engage in commercial ventures, driving economic growth and generating much-needed revenue for the crown.

The centralization of taxation and the implementation of more efficient revenue collection mechanisms bolstered the royal coffers, providing the resources necessary to fund the monarch's ambitious projects and initiatives. This influx of funds allowed Henry VII to invest in infrastructure, fortifications, and a professional bureaucracy, further strengthening his hold on power and laying the groundwork for the flourishing of the Tudor dynasty.

Moreover, the economic reforms served to curtail the influence of the nobility, as the crown's increased financial independence reduced its reliance on the feudal system. By consolidating control over taxation and trade, Henry VII effectively undermined the power base of the aristocracy, ensuring their allegiance and preventing potential challenges to his authority.

While the economic reforms benefited the kingdom as a whole, their impacts were not evenly distributed across society. The aristocracy, long accustomed to wielding significant influence and amassing vast wealth, found their fortunes threatened by the king's centralizing policies. As the crown sought to rein in the power of the nobility and assert its authority over taxation and trade, many noble families saw their revenues diminished and their privileges curtailed.

On the other hand, the common people experienced a mixed impact from the economic reforms. The stabilization of the currency and the promotion of trade and commerce fostered economic growth, creating new opportunities for merchants and tradesmen. However, the increased taxation and the crown's aggressive pursuit of revenue often placed a disproportionate burden on the lower classes, fueling resentment and discontent.

Despite these challenges, Henry VII's economic policies were pivotal in establishing a strong foundation for the Tudor dynasty and shaping the trajectory of England for generations to come. His strategic approach to taxation, trade, and currency regulation not only secured his political position but also set the stage for the nation's economic ascendancy, paving the way for the golden age that would follow under his successors.

In the aftermath of the tumultuous War of the Roses, Henry VII's economic reforms proved instrumental in rebuilding a realm torn asunder by years of conflict. By centralizing taxation, promoting trade, and stabilizing the currency, the prudent monarch addressed the kingdom's financial woes and laid the groundwork for future prosperity. These policies not only bolstered the royal coffers and cemented the Tudor dynasty's hold on power but also fostered economic growth and paved the way for England's emergence as a commercial and maritime powerhouse.

While the impacts of these reforms were not uniformly positive, with the aristocracy and common people experiencing varying degrees of benefit and hardship, the overarching legacy of Henry VII's economic strategy remains a testament to the enduring importance of sound financial governance. By skillfully interweaving economic policy with political statecraft, the king demonstrated the inextricable link between a nation's financial fortunes and its ability to project power and influence on the global stage.

As England embarked on a new era under the Tudor dynasty, Henry VII's economic reforms would reverberate through the centuries, shaping the nation's trajectory and serving as a blueprint for the strategic use of economic might in the pursuit of political ambitions. In the annals of English history, his reign stands as a pivotal moment when the power of the purse became inextricably tied to the power of the crown, forever altering the landscape of governance and paving the way for England's ascendancy as a global economic and political force.

Henry VII's Legacy of Marriage Alliances

In the realm of statecraft and diplomacy, few tools have proven as potent as the strategic marriage alliance. Transcending mere personal unions, these carefully orchestrated unions held the power to forge lasting bonds between nations, create intricate webs of political allegiances, and shape the destinies of entire dynasties. As the first Tudor monarch, Henry VII recognized the immense value of such marital diplomacy, deftly employing these unions in a manner that stood in stark contrast to the practices of his predecessors. While his approach may have appeared pragmatic, even opportunistic, it laid the foundation for a new era of international relations, one defined by strategic foresight and a profound understanding of the delicate balance of power.

In the tumultuous era preceding Henry VII's ascension, the pursuit of marriage alliances was often driven by personal ambition or short-term political expediency. The Plantagenet monarchs, embroiled in the bitter War of the Roses, sought to bolster their claims to the throne through matrimonial ties, forging alliances that were as fleeting as they were tenuous. These unions, born of necessity rather than strategic vision, did little to establish lasting bonds between nations or secure a stable line of succession.

Henry VII, however, approached these marriage alliances with a far more nuanced and calculated perspective. His aspirations extended beyond mere dynastic security; he sought to create diplomatic relations that would cement England's position on the European stage, safeguarding the realm from external threats and ensuring a lasting legacy for the newly established Tudor dynasty.

One of the monarch's most notable alliances was the union between his eldest son, Arthur, Prince of Wales, and the Spanish princess Catherine of Aragon. This momentous marriage, negotiated with the utmost care and precision, forged an unbreakable bond between the English and Spanish crowns, aligning two of the most formidable powers of the age. While the untimely death of Prince Arthur threatened to unravel this delicate arrangement, Henry VII's deft maneuvering ensured that the union would endure, paving the way for the eventual marriage between Catherine and his younger son, the future Henry VIII.

This strategic alliance not only secured England's position in the complex web of European politics but also laid the groundwork for the nation's future ascendancy as a global maritime and commercial powerhouse. Through Catherine's Spanish heritage and connections, the English gained access to the burgeoning trade networks and colonial enterprises that would fuel their economic prosperity in the centuries to come.

Yet Henry VII's diplomatic vision also looked closer to home. With a keen eye for the shifting dynamics of power across the continent, he sought to forge alliances that would counterbalance the influence of rival nations and safeguard England's interests. One such union was the betrothal of his eldest daughter, Margaret, to the Scottish king James IV. This carefully orchestrated match not only helped quell the longstanding hostilities between the two kingdoms but also secured England's northern borders, allowing the Tudor monarch to focus his attention on more pressing matters.

The outcomes of these strategic marriages reverberated throughout Europe, altering the delicate balance of power and influencing the course of history. The union and subsequent divorce between Catherine of Aragon and Henry VIII would ultimately lead to the English Reformation, forever reshaping the religious landscape of the realm and setting the stage for the nation's emergence as a Protestant bastion. Meanwhile, the progeny of Margaret's marriage to James IV would eventually unite the crowns of England and Scotland, paving the way for the creation of the unified Kingdom of Great Britain.

Yet, Henry VII's legacy in the realm of marital diplomacy extended far beyond the mere forging of alliances. His approach fundamentally transformed the very nature of international relations, elevating marriage from a mere personal affair to a matter of state. No longer were these unions viewed as mere dynastic transactions; they were meticulously crafted instruments of statecraft, wielded with precision and foresight to further the strategic interests of the realm.

In stark contrast to the often haphazard and reactionary practices of his predecessors, Henry VII's marriage alliances were the product of careful deliberation and long-term planning. Each union was painstakingly negotiated, with every detail scrutinized and every potential outcome weighed against the broader geopolitical landscape. This level of strategic thinking, coupled with a keen understanding of the intricate web of dynastic ties that bound the nations of Europe, allowed the Tudor monarch to navigate the treacherous waters of international politics with unparalleled dexterity.

As the repercussions of these matrimonial unions continue to echo through the annals of history, it becomes clear that

Henry VII's legacy extends far beyond the mere establishment of a new dynasty. His masterful use of marriage alliances not only secured his reign and safeguarded the future of the Tudor line but also ushered in a new era of diplomacy, one in which the personal and the political were inextricably intertwined. Through his visionary approach, the king laid the foundations for England's emergence as a global superpower, forging diplomatic ties that would shape the course of nations for centuries to come.

In the modern era, where international relations are governed by a complex web of treaties, alliances, and economic interdependencies, the legacy of Henry VII's marital diplomacy serves as a poignant reminder of the enduring power of strategic unions. While the dynamics of statecraft have evolved, the fundamental principles that guided the Tudor monarch's approach remain as relevant as ever – foresight, calculation, and an unwavering commitment to the pursuit of national interests. As nations continue to navigate the ever-shifting currents of global politics, the lessons imparted by Henry VII's masterful use of marriage alliances stand as a testament to the enduring importance of strategic thinking and diplomatic acumen in shaping the destinies of nations.

The Enduring Challenge: Curbing Aristocratic Power

Inheriting a realm that had been ravaged by years of civil strife, the new king recognized the pressing need to restore order, stability, and the preeminence of the crown. It was an arduous task, one that required a judicious blend of legal reforms, administrative measures, and a keen understanding of the delicate balance of power within the English nobility.

In this volatile landscape, where the vestiges of aristocratic resistance still lingered, Henry VII understood that a mere assertion of royal prerogative would prove insufficient. Instead, he embraced an evidence-based approach, carefully analyzing the root causes of the challenges he faced and crafting meticulously tailored solutions grounded in empirical data and historical precedent. This commitment to evidence-based governance would become a hallmark of his reign, guiding his efforts to curb the influence of the nobility and consolidate the Crown's authority.

Throughout the tumultuous history of English monarchy, the tension between royal authority and the ambitions of the noble classes had been a recurring theme. From the Magna Carta to the Wars of the Roses, the very fabric of governance had been shaped by the delicate dance between the Crown and its powerful subjects. Henry VII, acutely aware of this enduring challenge, recognized the need to curtail the influence of the aristocracy, lest their unchecked power undermine the stability of his newly established dynasty.

Henry VII embarked on a series of legal and administrative reforms that would reshape the very fabric of English governance. Chief among these initiatives was the development of the Court of Star Chamber, a judicial body that would prove pivotal in reining in the influence of the aristocracy.

The Star Chamber, derived its name from the latin "Camera Stellata " or the "Starred Chamber," and was a courtroom adorned with stars painted on the ceiling, lending it an air of celestial authority. Yet, its true significance lay in its composition and far-reaching powers. Comprised of members of the Privy Council and presided over by the Lord Chancellor, the Star

Chamber held jurisdiction over a wide range of offenses, from riots and perjury to the more nebulous charges of misconduct and contempt.

What distinguished the Star Chamber from traditional courts was its ability to circumvent the constraints of common law and the interference of juries, which were often susceptible to the influence of powerful nobles. Instead, the court relied on evidence gathered through rigorous investigations, coupled with the expertise of its esteemed members, to render verdicts that were grounded in reason and impartiality.

The impact of the Star Chamber on the balance of power within English governance was profound. No longer could the nobility rely on their traditional strongholds of influence to evade justice or defy the authority of the Crown. The court's powers and its reliance on empirical evidence ensured that even the mightiest lords were subject to the rule of law, setting a precedent that would resonate throughout the Tudor era and beyond.

If we were to narrow Henry VII's action in controling the gentry down to five simple points that combine what we have said so far they would be as following:

1. **Financial Control**: Henry VII implemented a policy of strict financial control over the nobility and gentry. He heavily relied on his ability to raise revenue through taxation, which gave him leverage over the wealthy landowners. By closely monitoring their finances and imposing heavy fines for any perceived infractions, Henry VII ensured that the gentry remained financially dependent on the crown.

2. **Court Intrigues and Surveillance**: Henry VII was known for his astute use of spies and informants to keep a close

watch on the activities of the nobility and gentry. This surveillance helped him identify and neutralize potential threats to his power, whether they were plotting against him or engaging in activities that could challenge royal authority.

3. **Acts of Attainder**: Henry VII used Acts of Attainder to legally strip nobles of their titles, lands, and privileges if they were suspected of treason or disloyalty. This not only punished individual offenders but also served as a deterrent to others who might contemplate defying the crown.

4. **Limiting Power Structures**: Henry VII strategically weakened the power structures that traditionally supported the gentry. For example, he reduced the authority of the nobility by promoting loyal commoners to positions of power and by limiting the influence of the nobility in the government.

5. **Strengthening Royal Authority**: Henry VII focused on consolidating and strengthening royal authority during his reign. He worked to centralize power in the hands of the monarchy and diminish the influence of regional power brokers, including the gentry. By asserting the supremacy of the crown, Henry VII aimed to diminish the autonomy of the gentry and ensure their loyalty to the throne.

Overall, Henry VII's policies aimed to curb the power of the gentry by exerting tight control over their finances, monitoring their activities, and limiting their ability to challenge royal authority. These measures were crucial in establishing the Tudor monarchy's control over England and laying the foundation for the centralized government that would characterize the Tudor era.

A New Era of English Diplomacy

In the tumultuous aftermath of the Wars of the Roses, as Henry VII sought to consolidate the Tudor dynasty's grip on power and restore order to a realm ravaged by civil conflict, a new era of English diplomacy was born. This period marked a profound shift in England's international standing, as the monarch and his advisors recognized the necessity of projecting a unified and formidable presence on the European stage, securing alliances and forging strategic partnerships that would solidify the nation's position among the great powers of the time.

While the concept of diplomacy was not a novel invention, its systematic application in pursuit of national interests can be traced back to the early years of Henry VII's reign. The roots of this new era can be found in the monarch's keen awareness of the importance of trade and the acquisition of knowledge, both of which would prove instrumental in shaping England's diplomatic endeavors.

The establishment of trade agreements with influential city-states like Florence and Venice laid the foundations for economic cooperation and the exchange of goods and ideas. Simultaneously, Henry VII recognized the value of espionage as a means of gathering intelligence and gaining insights into the machinations of rival powers. The deployment of agents and informants across Europe provided the monarch with a strategic advantage, enabling him to navigate the complex web of alliances and rivalries that defined the European political landscape.

Key Events and Milestones:

Treaty of Medina del Campo (1489): This treaty was signed between England and Spain. It established an alliance between

Henry VII and the Catholic Monarchs, Ferdinand II of Aragon and Isabella I of Castile. It included provisions for mutual defense and trade, strengthening England's position against France.

Treaty of Etaples (1492): Signed between Henry VII and King Charles VIII of France, this treaty ended the hostilities between England and France. It secured a yearly pension payment from France to England in exchange for Henry VII agreeing to withdraw English support for pretenders to the French throne.

Treaty of Perpetual Peace (1502): This treaty, also known as the Treaty of Richmond, was signed between England and Scotland. It established peace between the two kingdoms and included a marriage agreement between Henry VII's daughter Margaret Tudor and James IV of Scotland, which laid the groundwork for the union of the crowns of England and Scotland in the future.

These treaties played significant roles in shaping Henry VII's foreign policy and securing England's interests both domestically and internationally.

These treaties helped Henry VII consolidate his power, secure England's borders, and establish diplomatic relationships that would shape English foreign policy for years to come.

A Legacy of Balanced Governance

As the reign of Henry VII drew to a close, the impact of his evidence-based approach to governance and the reforms he implemented left an indelible mark on the English legal and political landscape. The Star Chamber, while not without its flaws and criticisms, had succeeded in curbing the unchecked power of the gentry and establishing the preeminence of the Crown's authority.

Yet, the true legacy of Henry VII's reforms extended far beyond the confines of his reign. By embracing an evidence-based approach and grounding his decisions in empirical data and historical precedent, he set a powerful example for his successors, laying the foundations for a more balanced and equitable system of governance.

The principles of impartiality, transparency, and the reliance on empirical evidence that underpinned the Star Chamber's proceedings would echo through the centuries, influencing the development of English law and inspiring future generations of jurists and lawmakers. While the court itself would eventually be abolished in 1641 AD a year before the start of the English Civil War, its lasting impact on the evolution of the English legal system would endure, shaping the very concept of the rule of law and the balance between individual liberties and the preservation of social order.

Moreover, Henry VII's efforts to curb the influence of the nobility and consolidate the authority of the Crown would have far-reaching consequences for the trajectory of English history. By establishing a strong, centralized monarchy capable of enforcing its will across the realm, he paved the way for the eventual emergence of England as a global superpower, with the Tudor and Stuart dynasties capitalizing on this foundation to project their influence far beyond the shores of the British Isles.

As we reflect on the legacy of Henry VII's reign, it becomes clear that his commitment to evidence-based governance and his judicious blend of legal reforms and administrative measures left an indelible mark on the fabric of English society. Through his unwavering pursuit of empirical data and his willingness to embrace innovative approaches, he not only navigated the challenges posed by the nobility but also set a precedent for a more balanced and equitable system of governance – one that would continue to evolve and adapt to the changing tides of history, ultimately shaping the very foundations of the modern legal and political order.

Henry VIII
Reign 1509-1547

The Young King: Early Years and Personal Ambitions

The ascendancy of Henry VIII to the throne in 1509 marked a dramatic shift in the course of English history, one that would see the nation irrevocably changed by the king's personal desires and his grand aspirations for England.

His reign, characterized by a series of matrimonial alliances, political maneuverings, and a significant religious upheaval, invites a closer analysis to understand the complexities inherent in his rule and its impact on the Tudor legacy.

Henry VIII's quest for a male heir is well-documented, driving much of his domestic and foreign policy.

His marriage to Catherine of Aragon in 1509 initially promised to solidify the Tudor claim to the throne and strengthen England's alliances on the European stage.

However, as the years passed without the birth of a male heir, the king's desperation grew, setting the stage for a series of events that would lead to one of the most significant religious transformations in English history.

- 1533: Henry's marriage to Catherine is annulled by Archbishop Cranmer five months after marrying Anne Boleyn in secret, marking the beginning of England's break with the Roman Catholic Church.

- 1534: The Act of Supremacy is passed, declaring Henry the Supreme Head of the Church of England.

This act not only severed ties with the Vatican but also redefined the religious landscape of England, ushering in the English Reformation.

- 1536-1541: The Dissolution of the Monasteries, under Henry's command, leads to the redistribution of church lands and wealth, significantly altering the socio-economic fabric of the nation.

Henry's marriages, particularly to Catherine of Aragon and later to Anne Boleyn, were not merely personal or political decisions; they were catalysts for a religious revolution that would challenge the very soul of England.

The king's pursuit of a male heir, intertwined with his desire for greater autonomy from Rome, propelled the nation into a period of religious and social tumult.

The establishment of the Church of England was a monumental shift, not just in ecclesiastical terms, but as a declaration of royal supremacy over spiritual matters, fundamentally altering the relationship between the crown and its subjects.

This period was also marked by significant cultural and intellectual shifts, as the dissolution of the monasteries and the establishment of the Church of England facilitated the spread of Renaissance and humanist ideas.

The royal court became a center for scholars, artists, and thinkers, contributing to a vibrant cultural scene that would lay the groundwork for the Elizabethan Age.

Yet, Henry's policies and actions were not without their detractors and consequences.

The suppression of the Pilgrimage of Grace, a widespread uprising against the dissolution of the monasteries, and the execution of key figures such as Thomas More, underscore the lengths to which Henry was willing to go to secure his objectives.

These actions, while ensuring the consolidation of Tudor power, also sowed the seeds of future conflicts and divisions.

The adaptation of Henry's policies across his reign, from his initial attempts to secure a male heir through diplomatic marriages to his ultimate break with the Catholic Church, reflects a ruler of immense ambition and complexity.

His actions reshaped England's religious institutions, influenced its cultural development, and redefined its place on the European stage.

As we proceed further into the narrative of Tudor England, we encounter a dynasty that navigated the treacherous currents of change with a blend of ruthlessness, vision, and adaptability.

Henry VIII's reign, with its dramatic marriages, religious upheaval, and cultural flowering, serves as a pivotal chapter in this story, offering insights into the personal ambitions and political realities that shaped the Tudor era.

It is within this intricate interplay of power, faith, and identity that we find the essence of Tudor England, a realm transformed by the actions of a king whose legacy continues to fascinate and provoke debate.

The Great Matter: Divorce, Reformation, and Schism

In the unfolding drama of Henry VIII's reign, the establishment of the Church of England was not merely a capricious act of royal authority; it was a calculated maneuver that underscored the intricate relationship between power, religion, and governance in Tudor England. This seismic shift in the ecclesiastical landscape propelled the nation into uncharted theological and political territories, raising profound questions about the nature of sovereignty and the locus of spiritual authority.

1536: The Ten Articles are promulgated, defining the doctrine of the newly established Church of England and beginning the theological divergence from Roman Catholicism.

The ramifications of these actions extended far beyond the immediate context of Henry's reign. The dissolution of the monasteries, for example, was not only an attack on the wealth and power of the Catholic Church but also a profound realignment of England's socio-economic structure. The redistribution of church lands facilitated the rise of a new class of gentry, altering the dynamics of power and patronage within the kingdom. This, in turn, laid the groundwork for shifts in agricultural practices, urbanization, and the gradual emergence of a capitalist economy.

The theological underpinnings of the Church of England, began to evolve under the influence of Protestant reformers. The publication of the Great Bible in 1539, the first authorized edition in English, marked a pivotal moment in this transformation, making the scriptures accessible to a broader audience and encouraging the spread of Protestant beliefs.

Henry's establishment of the Church of England also had profound implications for the arts and culture. The monarch's patronage of scholars, poets, and musicians fostered an environment in which the arts could flourish, albeit within the parameters of the new religious orthodoxy. The dissolution of the monasteries, while devastating to the monastic communities, inadvertently led to the dispersal of their libraries and the spread of classical and humanist learning.

This period of religious and cultural upheaval was not without its challenges. The Act of Six Articles in 1539, which reaffirmed many traditional Catholic doctrines such as transubstantiation and clerical celibacy, highlighted the tensions and contradictions within the nascent Church of England. These tensions would continue to simmer throughout Henry's reign and beyond, contributing to the religious conflicts that would plague England for generations. Not until 1547, under Henry's son Edward, would the Act of Six Articles be repealed.

Furthermore, the establishment of the Church of England set a precedent for the role of the monarchy in religious affairs, a precedent that would have lasting consequences for the relationship between church and state. The notion that the king could, by decree, determine the religious life of his subjects was a radical departure from medieval conceptions of kingship and papal authority, raising questions about the limits of royal power and the nature of religious freedom.

As we delve deeper into the complexities of Henry VIII's reign, we are confronted with a monarch whose actions reshaped the religious, political, and cultural landscapes of his kingdom. His establishment of the Church of England was a bold assertion of royal authority over spiritual matters, but it was also a reflection of the broader currents of change that were sweeping across Europe during the Renaissance and Reformation. This moment of transformation, fraught with contradiction and conflict, offers a fascinating lens through which to examine the interplay of power, belief, and identity in Tudor England.

The legacy of Henry VIII, therefore, is not merely one of dynastic ambition or religious reform; it is a testament to the enduring impact of individual decisions on the course of history. As we continue our exploration of the Tudor era, we must grapple with the complexities of a period that was marked by profound shifts in the way that power was conceived, exercised, and resisted. It is within this turbulent context that the story of Tudor England unfolds, revealing the multifaceted nature of human ambition and the intricacy of historical change.

The Later Years: Matrimonial Politics and Royal Intrigues

Throughout Henry VIII's reign, his matrimonial alliances serve as pivotal chapters, each marriage not only a personal union but a strategic maneuver with far-reaching implications for the kingdom. As time went on, the kings patience wearied with his queen and lack of a male heir. Anne Boleyn was executed on May 19, 1536, primarily due to charges of treason, adultery, and incest brought against her. The circumstances leading to her execution are complex and intertwined with political and personal motives of the time:

1.Failure to Produce a Male Heir: Anne Boleyn's marriage to King Henry VIII of England was initially motivated by Henry's desire to annul his marriage to Catherine of Aragon, which had not produced a male heir. Anne's failure to give birth to a male heir created tension and dissatisfaction within the royal court.

2.Political Intrigues and Enemies: Anne Boleyn had accumulated enemies at court, including factions that were loyal to Henry's previous wife, Catherine of Aragon. These enemies worked to undermine Anne's position and credibility.

3. Charges of Adultery and Incest: Anne was accused of committing adultery with several men, including her alleged lovers, among them her own brother, George Boleyn. These charges were likely fabricated or exaggerated to damage her reputation and influence.

4. Henry's Desire for a New Marriage: By 1536, Henry had become infatuated with Jane Seymour, one of Anne's ladies-in-waiting. Anne's failure to produce a male heir and the political tensions surrounding her meant that Henry sought to end his marriage with her.

5. Legal Proceedings and Trial: Anne was arrested in 1536 and charged with adultery, incest, and plotting to kill the king. She was tried by a court that was heavily influenced by her enemies. She was found guilty and subsequently executed by beheading.

In summary, Anne Boleyn's execution was a result of a combination of factors including her failure to produce a male heir, the political intrigues and machinations at court, and Henry VIII's desire for a new marriage. The charges of treason, adultery, and incest were used as a means to remove her from power and facilitate Henry's pursuit of a new wife.

After the seismic shifts brought about by his marriage to Anne Boleyn and the establishment of the Church of England, Henry's marital saga continued with Jane Seymour, a union that would bring the king closer to his long-coveted male heir.

1536: Henry marries Jane Seymour mere days after Anne Boleyn's execution, a swift move that underscores the king's urgency to secure a Tudor male succession.

1537: The birth of Edward VI, Henry's long-desired male heir, momentarily solidifies the Tudor dynasty's future, fulfilling Henry's quest for a legitimate son to inherit the throne.

Jane Seymour's tenure as queen consort, though brief, marked a period of relative calm and consolidation in Henry's reign. Her ability to deliver a male heir endeared her to the king and momentarily quelled the succession crises that had plagued the Tudor court.

However, her untimely death in 1537, just days after Edward's birth, plunged Henry into a deep mourning that would have significant implications for his subsequent marriages and the political landscape of the kingdom.

The years following Jane's death saw Henry's marital endeavors become increasingly intertwined with the political machinations and religious transformations of his reign.

His subsequent marriages—to Anne of Cleves, Catherine Howard, and finally Catherine Parr—were marked by a complex interplay of diplomatic considerations, personal desires, and religious policy.

1540: Henry marries Anne of Cleves in January. By July his annulment to her is complete, citing that they never consumated the marriage. Reports state that Henry found her ugly and nothing at all like her portrait. Just nineteen days after his annulment, Henry marries Catherine Howard, a maid of honor to Anne of Cleves, the same month. Notably Catherine is believed to have been only ninteen, leaving a thirty year age gap between them.

1542: Catherine Howard's execution for treason and adultery highlights the perilous nature of Tudor court life and the stringent expectations placed upon queens consort.

1543: Henry's marriage to Catherine Parr ushers in a period of relative stability and sees the return of Henry's daughters, Mary and Elizabeth, to the line of succession, an act that would have profound implications for the future of the Tudor dynasty.

Catherine Parr's influence on Henry, particularly in matters of religion, contributed to a subtle but significant shift in the king's policies.

Her advocacy for the Protestant cause and her role in reconciling Henry with his daughters from previous marriages helped to stabilize the Tudor succession and mitigate the religious tensions that had characterized much of Henry's reign.

As Henry's health declined and his reign neared its end, the political landscape of England continued to evolve, shaped by the king's marital decisions and the religious reforms he had initiated.

The succession of his son, Edward VI, would mark the beginning of a new chapter in Tudor history, one characterized by ambitious Protestant reforms and the further entrenchment of the Church of England as a national institution.

The legacy of Henry VIII's later reign, with its marriages, religious upheaval, and political maneuvering, offers a compelling lens through which to examine the interplay of personal ambition and public policy.

It is a testament to the ways in which the actions of a single individual can ripple through the annals of history, influencing the course of national destiny and shaping the collective memory of a nation.

In navigating the intricacies of Henry VIII's matrimonial and political strategies, we are offered a vivid glimpse into the Tudor court's power dynamics, the shifting allegiances, and the personal ambitions that drove the kingdom's evolution.

This exploration not only deepens our understanding of Henry VIII's reign but also illuminates the broader currents of change that swept through Tudor England, forever altering its cultural, religious, and political landscape.

Religion and Reformation

A Deeper look at why Henry VIII Broke With Rome

Of all the changes that Henry VIII enacted from ascending to the throne 1509, few changed the face of English history as did the break with the Roman Catholic Church in 1534. Why did Henry VIII, a once devout Catholic monarch, radically transform the religious landscape of England by establishing the Church of England? This question not only piques curiosity but beckons us into a labyrinth of power, passion, and politics that defined the Tudor era. Understanding the motivations behind such a monumental shift is crucial, for it was a decision that would forever alter the course of English history and religion. The establishment of the Church of England is not merely a tale of a king seeking a male heir but a complex story of ambition, defiance, and a desperate quest for sovereignty and legacy. To fully grasp the magnitude of this question, we must delve into the intricacies of the period. Henry's decision was not made in isolation; it was the culmination of years of frustration, personal desires, and geopolitical pressures. The problem at the heart of our exploration is multifaceted, involving issues of marital politics, theological disputes, and the struggle for autonomy against the powerful Roman Catholic Church. The complications were numerous, including the Pope's refusal to annul Henry's marriage to Catherine of Aragon, the influence of the Reformation sweeping across Europe, and Henry's obsession with securing a male successor to stabilize the Tudor dynasty.

Common misconceptions often simplify this narrative to Henry's lust or his tyrannical quest for power. While these elements played a role, they overshadow the broader, more complex motivations. Traditional approaches to this historical event frequently focus on the sensational aspects of Henry's reign, such as his six marriages or the dissolution of the monasteries, without fully engaging with the political, religious, and personal dilemmas faced by the king. Our unique approach seeks to contextualize Henry's decision within the broader socio-political and religious upheavals of the 16th century. By examining the confluence of personal, domestic, and international factors, we offer a more nuanced understanding of why the Church of England was established. This perspective acknowledges Henry's personal desires but also considers the strategic considerations that influenced his decision, including the desire for national sovereignty, the influence of the Reformation, and the economic benefits of breaking from Rome. For instance, the case of Thomas Cranmer, Archbishop of Canterbury, illustrates how Henry's religious policies were not solely driven by personal vendettas but were also influenced by theological and political considerations. Cranmer's support for the annulment of Henry's marriage and his subsequent role in establishing the Church of England highlight the intricate interplay between personal motivations and wider political and religious reforms. Skeptics might argue that attributing such complex motivations to Henry simplifies the role of key figures like Anne Boleyn or Thomas Cromwell, or underestimates the influence of the Reformation itself. However, by dissecting these motivations and examining the broader context, we can appreciate the multifaceted nature of Henry's decision. This approach does not diminish the impact of these figures or movements but rather situates them within a larger narrative that considers a wide range of influences. To apply this perspective to our understanding of history, readers are encouraged to explore primary sources from the period, such as letters, treaties, and religious texts, to gain insights into the myriad factors that influenced Henry's decision. Additionally, engaging with scholarship that examines the political, religious, and economic contexts of the 16th century can provide a fuller picture of the era. By adopting a holistic approach to history, we can move beyond simplistic explanations and appreciate the complexity of the past. In doing so, we not only deepen our understanding of a pivotal moment in history but also enhance our ability to analyze and interpret the myriad factors that drive historical change. This method allows us to see beyond the surface of historical events and grasp the nuanced motivations and consequences that shape our world.

The Act of Supremacy: Defining Moments

Understanding the key terms and concepts surrounding the Act of Supremacy is pivotal in grasping the profound shift it signified in the religious and political landscape of England. These terms not only illuminate the intricacies of the period but also serve as a beacon, guiding us through the convoluted interplay between religious authority and royal power. In our exploration, we will dissect terms such as 'Supreme Head', 'Church of England', and 'Act of Supremacy' itself, each a cornerstone in comprehending the magnitude of the changes enacted during Henry VIII's reign. Through these lenses, we will delve into the historical, political, and theological undercurrents that shaped this pivotal moment in history. Transitioning into our detailed examination, the forthcoming discussion will revolve around the aforementioned terms. This structured approach not only aids in a systematic exploration but also primes the reader for a deeper understanding of the multifaceted dynamics at play.

Firstly, the term 'Supreme Head' requires unpacking. Historically, this title, as conferred upon Henry VIII, marked a radical departure from centuries of papal supremacy over the church in England. By adopting this title, Henry effectively asserted his authority over the English church, sidelining the Pope. This move was not merely a change in religious oversight but symbolized a profound realignment of power, placing the monarchy at the pinnacle of England's spiritual hierarchy. The implications were monumental, signaling the beginning of a new era wherein the crown wielded unprecedented control over religious affairs.

Next, 'Church of England' is a term that encapsulates the institution born out of Henry's break with Rome. Prior to the Act of Supremacy, the church in England was a part of the broader Roman Catholic Church. The establishment of the Church of England marked the creation of a national church under the direct jurisdiction of the English monarchy. This was a transformative moment, redefining the religious identity of the nation and laying the groundwork for future religious reformations and conflicts within England and between England and other nations.

Lastly, the 'Act of Supremacy' itself, enacted in 1534, legally established the king's status as the supreme head of the Church of England. This act not only formalized the break with the Roman Catholic Church but also required an oath of loyalty from English subjects to recognize this supremacy. The act's passage was a clear manifestation of the intertwining of governance and religion, underscoring the monarchy's dominance over spiritual matters and furthering the centralization of power.By reflecting on these terms, one can draw parallels with contemporary issues of governance, religion, and the centralization of power. These reflections not only enrich our understanding of the past but also offer insightful perspectives on current debates surrounding the role of religion in state affairs and the boundaries of authority. Linking these defined terms to the broader narrative of the book, we see how the Act of Supremacy was not an isolated incident but a culmination of tensions and aspirations that had been brewing for centuries. It represents a watershed moment, not only in the religious history of England but also in the evolution of modern nation-states, where the lines between religious and political authority were redrawn. As we move forward, these concepts will serve as a foundation for exploring the cascading effects of the Act of Supremacy on subsequent developments in English history and beyond.

The Dissolution of the Monasteries: An Economic and Social Shift

In the mid-16th century, England witnessed one of the most transformative periods in its ecclesiastical and socio-economic landscape - the Dissolution of the Monasteries. Under the aegis of King Henry VIII, this movement saw the disbanding and demolition of monastic institutions across the country, a decision that would have far-reaching consequences for English society and its economy.The main players in this historical narrative include King Henry VIII, who initiated the dissolution, his chief minister Thomas Cromwell, who orchestrated the process, and the monastic institutions themselves, which had been integral to English society for centuries. These establishments were not only places of worship but also centers of education, healthcare, and landownership.The primary issue at hand was the considerable wealth and land held by the monasteries, which the crown sought to control. This challenge was significant because it represented a drastic shift in power dynamics, from religious institutions to the monarchy and lay landowners. The dissolution was also motivated by Henry's desire to consolidate his authority and break away from the Papal authority of the Roman Catholic Church, establishing the Church of England in its stead.To address this challenge, the Crown employed a systematic approach. Initially, it conducted detailed surveys (Valor Ecclesiasticus) to assess the wealth of the monasteries. Following this, acts of Parliament were passed to legalize the dissolution process. Monasteries were then either voluntarily surrendered to the crown in exchange for pensions or forcibly taken over. The properties were sold off or granted to loyal nobles and merchants, fundamentally altering the ownership and use of vast tracts of land.The outcomes of these actions were profound. The Crown significantly increased its revenue and land holdings. The redistribution of monastic lands contributed to the rise of a new class of gentry and the commercialization of agriculture, which would later fuel the Agricultural Revolution. However, the dissolution also led to the loss of many services provided by the monasteries, such as education, healthcare, and hospitality to travelers, pushing these responsibilities onto local parishes and nascent charitable institutions. This illustrates the complexities of disrupting established social and economic structures. While the dissolution facilitated the consolidation of royal power and the reformation of religious practices, it also precipitated social upheaval and economic shifts. The immediate economic benefits to the Crown and its supporters contrast with the long-term challenges of providing social services and managing agricultural productivity. The Dissolution of the Monasteries is a pivotal event that underscores the interplay between power, religion, and economics in shaping society. It highlights the consequences of centralizing power and redistributing wealth, offering insights into the transformative impact of policy decisions on the fabric of society. This not only sheds light on a critical period of English history but also serves as a reminder of the enduring effects of institutional and economic reforms. As we reflect on the dissolution's legacy, it is worth considering how the redistribution of resources and the reconfiguration of societal roles continue to influence contemporary debates about wealth, power, and social responsibility.

Catholicism Vs. Protestantism: The Tudor Dilemma

The tumultuous reigns of the Tudor monarchs present a fascinating study of contrasting religious policies that shaped England's spiritual landscape. This period, marked by profound changes and enduring legacies, offers a unique lens through which to explore the complex interplay between religion and power. By comparing tund contrasting the religious policies of Henry VIII, Edward VI, Mary I, and Elizabeth I, we can gain deeper insights into the motivations, consequences, and broader themes underlying these shifts. The purpose here is not only to delineate the historical facts but to understand the significance of these religious oscillations in the context of governance, personal belief, and societal impact. Specifically, we will examine the doctrinal orientations, enforcement strategies, and the relationship with Rome under each monarch, shedding light on the similarities and differences that characterize their reigns. The similarities between the Tudor monarchs often lie beneath the surface, obscured by their more overt divergences. For instance, despite their differing religious affiliations, each monarch utilized religion as a tool for consolidating power and legitimizing their rule. From Henry VIII's break with Rome to Elizabeth I's establishment of the Church of England, religion served as a means to an end, a mechanism for unifying the nation under the sovereign's control. Furthermore, each monarch faced and responded to significant opposition, whether from within the country or from the papacy, highlighting the constant tension between religious policy and political stability. The differences, however, are more pronounced and have had lasting impacts on English history. Henry VIII's establishment of the Church of England marked a dramatic departure from the Catholic Church, setting the stage for subsequent religious reforms. Edward VI continued on this path, further entrenching Protestant doctrines. In stark contrast, Mary I sought to reverse these changes, reinstating Roman Catholicism and earning the nickname 'Bloody Mary' for her persecution of Protestants. Elizabeth I navigated a middle path with the Elizabethan Religious Settlement, seeking to pacify religious tensions while establishing a Protestant church that retained some Catholic elements. These differences in religious policy reveal broader themes of authority, identity, and conflict. The Tudor period exemplifies the challenges of governing a religiously divided nation and the lengths to which rulers will go to secure their power and legacy. The fluctuating religious landscape under the Tudors also underscores the pivotal role of individual monarchs in shaping national religion, highlighting the personal nature of the Reformation in England. Moreover, the enduring impact of these policies is evident in the religious diversity and tensions that persist in England today, making the Tudor era not only a historical curiosity but a relevant lens for understanding contemporary issues of religious freedom, state control, and identity politics. In examining the religious policies of the Tudor monarchs, we uncover a tapestry of ambition, faith, and strife that continues to influence the modern world.

Edward VI
Reign 1547-1553

The Boy King: Reforming England

As we transition from the tumultuous yet transformative reign of Henry VIII to that of his son, Edward VI, we are presented with a starkly different chapter in the Tudor narrative. Edward's accession to the throne in 1547, at the tender age of nine, inaugurated a period dominated not by the forceful personality of a king, but by the ambitious agendas of his regents and the rapid advancement of Protestant reforms.

1547: Edward VI's reign begins, under the regency of Edward Seymour, Duke of Somerset, who embarks on a series of radical Protestant reforms.

1549: The Act of Uniformity is passed, mandating the use of the Book of Common Prayer in services and solidifying the English Reformation's break from Catholic liturgical practices.

1550: Somerset's fall from power and the rise of John Dudley, Duke of Northumberland, who continues the Protestant agenda but with a more politically astute approach.

Edward VI's reign, though brief, was a crucible of religious change, with the young king himself a devout Protestant, keenly interested in the religious affairs of his kingdom. The introduction of the Book of Common Prayer, the enforcement of the Act of Uniformity, and the aggressive dismantling of Catholic practices underpinned a move towards a more distinctly English form of Protestantism. These reforms, while consolidating the religious shifts initiated by Henry VIII, also provoked resistance and unrest, as seen in the Prayer Book Rebellion of 1549.

The governance under Edward's regency was marked by a blend of religious zealotry and political maneuvering. Somerset's initial control was characterized by ambitious social and religious reforms aimed at improving the lot of the common people and purifying the church. However, his failure to manage the kingdom's finances and his handling of foreign policy, particularly the costly war with Scotland, led to his downfall.

The subsequent rise of Northumberland shifted the focus somewhat from religious reform to political consolidation. Northumberland's regime was more pragmatic, focusing on strengthening the position of the monarchy and ensuring the continuation of Protestant reforms. His ultimate maneuver, the attempt to place Lady Jane Grey on the throne to avoid a Catholic succession, epitomizes the political calculations that underpinned the governance of Edward's reign.

Edward VI's health, always fragile, deteriorated rapidly in early 1553, leading to his death and the brief, tumultuous reign of Lady Jane Grey before Mary I's accession.

The reign of Edward VI, though often overshadowed by the more dramatic periods of his father and sister, was a pivotal moment in the consolidation of the English Reformation. It was a time of fervent religious debate, significant liturgical change, and the strengthening of the royal supremacy over the church. The policies and reforms of this period would have lasting impacts, shaping the religious landscape of England and setting the stage for the complex religious politics of Mary I's and Elizabeth I's reigns.

Edward's reign illustrates the profound impact that regency governance can have on the trajectory of a nation, especially when coupled with the fervor of religious reform. The young king's devoutness, combined with the ambitions of his regents, propelled England further down the path of Protestantism, embedding it more deeply in the national identity. This period of significant transformation, driven by a combination of personal belief and political expediency, underscores the intricate dynamics of power, faith, and governance in Tudor England.

As the narrative of Tudor England unfolds, the reign of Edward VI offers a compelling study of how youth, ambition, and religious conviction can intersect with the mechanisms of governance to forge a new path for a nation. It is a testament to the enduring influence of the Tudors, not only in shaping the political and religious contours of England but also in setting the stage for the challenges and achievements of subsequent reigns.

Succession and Legacy: Edward's Impact on Tudor England

The ascendancy of Lady Jane Grey, albeit fleeting, represents a pivotal moment in the Tudor narrative, embodying the turbulent intersection of political ambition, religious ideology, and the quest for power.

Her nine-day reign in 1553, often referred to as a 'footnote' in English history, offers a profound lens through which to examine the fragility of monarchical power and the volatile nature of succession during the Tudor period.

1553: The designation of Lady Jane Grey as successor by Edward VI, in a bid to ensure the continuation of Protestant rule, underscores the depth of religious and political divisions within Tudor England.

Edward's decision, influenced by the Duke of Northumberland and enshrined in his 'Devise for the Succession', reflects not only the young king's devout Protestantism but also the machinations of those who sought to maintain their power and influence through the manipulation of succession.

Lady Jane's accession to the throne, though brief, was marked by a complex web of intrigue and ambition.

Her proclamation as queen, orchestrated by the Duke of Northumberland, was a calculated move that sought to circumvent the legitimate claims of Mary Tudor, Edward's Catholic half-sister.

This act of political maneuvering, however, quickly unraveled, as support for Mary's claim solidified, leading to Jane's deposition and the subsequent restoration of Catholic rule under Mary I.

The tragic outcome of Jane's reign, culminating in her execution in 1554, serves as a stark reminder of the perils inherent in the Tudor succession and the ruthless nature of power struggles within the monarchy.

Her brief tenure illuminates the complexities of governance in a period characterized by religious strife, dynastic rivalry, and the shifting allegiances of the nobility.

Moreover, the transition from Edward VI to Lady Jane Grey, and ultimately to Mary I, highlights the broader implications for England's religious landscape.

The tumultuous shifts in monarchical power during this period were emblematic of the deeper religious transformations sweeping across Europe, a reflection of the contentious battle between Protestantism and Catholicism that defined much of the sixteenth century.

The reign of Lady Jane Grey, though often overshadowed by the more prolonged and impactful reigns of her Tudor counterparts, offers valuable insights into the dynamics of succession, the interplay between religion and politics, and the challenges of female rulership in a male-dominated society.

The Nine Days' Queen: Lady Jane Grey

Reign 1553

The Religious Reckoning: Protestantism and Power

In 16th-century England, the threads of religious turmoil and political ambition were inextricably woven, creating a complex narrative where the quest for power and the pursuit of faith collided.

At the heart of this clash stood the figure of Lady Jane Grey, a young woman thrust into the maelstrom of Tudor succession politics, her fate intertwined with the rise of Protestantism and the struggle for religious supremacy.

One cannot fully comprehend the events surrounding Lady Jane's ascension to the throne without acknowledging the stark contrast between the Reformation's sweeping tide and the tenacity of the Catholic faith that had dominated England for centuries.

On one hand, the Protestant movement, fueled by the fervor of men like the Duke of Northumberland, sought to uproot the traditions of the past and usher in a new era of religious reform.

On the other, the steadfast adherents of Catholicism, embodied by Mary Tudor, clung fiercely to the rituals and doctrines that had shaped England's spiritual identity for generations.

This contrast between the reformist zeal of Protestantism and the unwavering devotion to Catholic tradition was not onlya theological debate; it was a clash of ideologies that reverberated through the corridors of power, shaping the course of history.

For Northumberland and his allies, Lady Jane Grey's ascension represented a pivotal moment, a chance to cement the Protestant faith's dominance and secure their own political ambitions.

In their eyes, the young Queen was a symbol of the new order, a figurehead for the cause they had embraced with fervent conviction.

Yet, even as they sought to elevate Lady Jane to the throne, the forces of tradition and Catholic loyalism remained steadfast.

Mary Tudor, the rightful heir according to many, embodied the resistance to this Protestant tide, her claim rooted in the very foundations of England's religious heritage.

As the news of Lady Jane's proclamation spread, the contrast between these opposing currents became ever more stark, with allegiances shifting and loyalties tested.

Beneath this religious upheaval lay the undercurrents of political ambition and power struggles that had long defined the Tudor dynasty.

Northumberland's machinations, while shrouded in religious reform, were ultimately likely also driven by a desire to consolidate his own position and influence.

Lady Jane, caught in the midst of this maelstrom, was but a pawn in a game of thrones, her ascension a means to an end for those who sought to shape the course of history to their own advantage.

As the events unfolded, the contrast between the lofty ideals of religious reformation and the harsh realities of political expediency became increasingly stark.

It was in this tumultuous landscape that Lady Jane Grey's reign unfolded, her brief tenure a fleeting moment in a broader struggle for religious and political dominance.

Her deposition and Mary's ascension signaled a shift in the tides, a triumph of tradition over the forces of reform, at least for a time.

Yet, the echoes of this conflict would reverberate through the years to come, shaping the course of England's religious and political landscape for generations.

The Fall of Lady Jane Grey: A Nine-Day Reign

Understanding the Fall of Lady Jane Grey's Nine-Day Reign: A Timeline of Events

The nine-day reign of Lady Jane Grey stands as a pivotal moment in English history, illustrating the intricate interplay between religious fervor, political ambition, and the shifting tides of power. Tracing the events leading to her deposition and subsequent imprisonment offers a compelling glimpse into the complex dynamics that shaped England's tumultuous path during the Tudor era.

- 1553: As Edward VI's health deteriorates, the question of succession looms large, with Northumberland and his allies determined to prevent the Catholic Mary Tudor from ascending to the throne and undoing the religious reforms.

- June 6, 1553: Edward VI, on his deathbed, is persuaded by Northumberland to alter the line of succession, bypassing his half-sisters Mary and Elizabeth in favor of Lady Jane Grey, the great-granddaughter of Henry VII and a devout Protestant.

- July 6, 1553: Edward VI dies, and Lady Jane Grey is proclaimed Queen at the age of sixteen, her reign backed by Northumberland and his supporters.

- July 10, 1553: Mary Tudor, aware of the plot against her, rallies support from Catholic nobles and gentry, prompting the defection of key supporters from Lady Jane's cause.

- July 19, 1553: Mary's forces enter London, and Lady Jane Grey's reign effectively ends after only nine days, with her removal from the throne and subsequent imprisonment in the Tower of London.

The Shifting Tides: Mary I's Consolidation of Power and the Catholic Revival

- July 25, 1553: Mary I is officially crowned Queen of England at Westminster Abbey, signaling the begin of the reversal of the Protestant reforms initiated during Edward VI's reign.

- August 1553 - November 1554: Mary I begins the process of restoring Catholicism as the established religion in England, appointing Catholic bishops, repealing Protestant legislation, and seeking to reunite the English Church with Rome.

- November 1553: Lady Jane Grey and her husband, Lord Guildford Dudley, are charged with high treason for their involvement in the attempt to usurp Mary's claim to the throne.

The Execution of Lady Jane Grey and the Aftermath

- February 12, 1554: Lady Jane Grey and her husband are executed on Tower Green after initially being pardoned, their deaths serving as a stark warning against further challenges to Mary I's authority.

- 1554-1558: Mary I's reign is marked by the reversal of Protestant reforms, the burning of religious dissenters (earning her the moniker 'Bloody Mary'), and the restoration of England's allegiance to the Roman Catholic Church through her marriage to Philip II of Spain.

The fall of Lady Jane Grey, though brief, represented a pivotal moment in the religious and political struggles that defined the Tudor era. Her deposition and subsequent execution served as a testament to the precarious nature of power, the fragility of alliances, and the willingness of those in authority to employ drastic measures in defense of their convictions.

Furthermore, the events surrounding Lady Jane's nine-day reign highlighted the deep divisions within English society, where religious loyalty and political ambition became intertwined, fueling conflicts that would reverberate for generations. Her story stands as a poignant reminder of the sacrifices made in the name of faith and ideology, and the enduring impact of these struggles on the shaping of nations and the course of history.

Trial and Execution: The End of a Tudor Tragedy

The tragic trial, imprisonment, and execution of Lady Jane Grey stand as a pivotal moment in Tudor history, encapsulating the era's complex interplay of religion, politics, and the pursuit of power. By examining the available historical evidence, we gain insight into the legal proceedings that led to Jane's demise, her remarkable conduct in the face of death, and the broader implications for notions of justice and mercy within the Tudor realm. An evidence-based approach is crucial in this context, as it allows us to separate fact from fiction, distill the truth from the myriad of accounts and interpretations, and gain a nuanced understanding of this profound historical episode.

This analysis aims to demonstrate that Lady Jane Grey's trial and execution, although shrouded in political machinations and religious tensions, ultimately reflect the tragic consequences of power struggles within the Tudor dynasty, and the unyielding application of the law, even in the face of mitigating circumstances and pleas for mercy.

The primary source of evidence lies in the meticulous records of Jane's trial proceedings, as documented in the 'Baga de Secretis' (Bag of Secrets), a collection of legal documents from the Tudor era. These records provide a detailed account of the charges leveled against Jane, the testimonies presented, and the eventual verdict and sentencing.

The 'Baga de Secretis' was a repository maintained by the Court of King's Bench, housing legal documents of significant importance. The records pertaining to Jane Grey's trial were meticulously kept, with verbatim transcripts of the proceedings, witness testimonies, and the judges' rulings. These documents are considered highly credible, as they were official court records subject to rigorous scrutiny and verification.

Jane was charged with high treason for her role in the attempted usurpation of the throne by her supporters, who aimed to prevent the accession of the rightful heir, Mary I. The prosecution presented evidence of Jane's complicity in the plot, arguing that she had knowingly accepted the crown and participated in efforts to resist Mary's claim to the throne.

Contemporaneous accounts from Jane's supporters and sympathizers suggest that she was an unwitting pawn in the larger power struggle orchestrated by her father-in-law, the Duke of Northumberland, and other Protestant advisors. These accounts argue that Jane, a mere teenager at the time, was coerced into accepting the crown and had little agency in the unfolding events.

While Jane's youth and potential coercion cannot be discounted, the legal records indicate that she was fully aware of the implications of her actions. During her trial, Jane acknowledged her role in the attempted usurpation, stating, 'I confess myself guilty of having consented to the thing, and allowed the fact, but not with my good will.' This admission, recorded in the court transcripts, suggests that she comprehended the gravity of her actions, even if she did not initiate or orchestrate the plot herself.

Furthermore, Jane's conduct during her imprisonment and execution demonstrated a remarkable resolve and acceptance of her fate, belying the notion that she was a mere pawn. Her eloquent and defiant speech on the scaffold, as documented by eyewitness accounts, revealed her unwavering commitment to her Protestant faith and her willingness to embrace martyrdom for her beliefs.

Additional evidence can be found in the letters exchanged between Jane and her family members during her imprisonment. These personal correspondences, preserved in various archives, offer a poignant glimpse into Jane's mindset and resolve as she awaited her fate.

In a letter to her sister, Lady Katherine Grey, Jane wrote:

'Now as touching my death, rejoice as I do, my dearest sister, that I shall be delivered of this corruption, and put on incorruption: for I am assured that I shall, for losing of a mortal life, win one that is immortal, joyful, and everlasting: the which I pray God grant you in his most blessed hour, and send you his all-saving grace to love in his fear, and to die in the true Christian faith: from which in God's name I exhort you that you never swerve, neither through hope of life, not fear of death: for if you will deny his truth, to give length to a weary and corrupt breath, God himself will deny you, and by vengeance make short what you by your soul's loss would prolong: but if you will cleave to him, he will stretch forth your days to an uncircumscribed comfort, and to his own glory: to the which glory, God bring me now, and you hereafter, when is shall please him to call you. Farewell once again, my beloved sister, and put your only trust in God, who only must help you. Amen.'

This remarkable stoicism and acceptance of her impending execution further reinforce the notion that Jane embraced her fate with remarkable composure and conviction.

The evidence surrounding Lady Jane Grey's trial and execution serves as a sobering reminder of the uncompromising application of the law during the Tudor era, even in the face of mitigating circumstances and pleas for mercy. It underscores the precarious nature of power and the willingness of those in authority to wield the full force of the law to maintain their hold on the throne.

Furthermore, Jane's defiant embrace of her Protestant faith and her refusal to renounce her beliefs, even when faced with execution, cemented her status as a martyr for the Protestant cause. Her tragic fate resonated deeply with the burgeoning

Protestant movement, fueling the ongoing religious tensions and conflicts that would shape the Tudor era and beyond.

In a broader context, the evidence surrounding Jane's trial and execution serves as a cautionary tale about the perils of political ambition and the consequences of becoming entangled in the machinations of those seeking power. It highlights the vulnerability of individuals caught in the crosshairs of these power struggles, even when they may not be the primary instigators.

Ultimately, Lady Jane Grey's trial and execution stand as a poignant historical episode that encapsulates the complex interplay of religion, politics, and the pursuit of power that defined the Tudor era. By examining the available evidence through a rigorous, evidence-based approach, we gain a deeper understanding of the legal proceedings, Jane's remarkable conduct in the face of adversity, and the broader implications for notions of justice and mercy within the Tudor realm.

Mary I
Reign 1553-1558
Restoration of Catholicism and Conflict

The Catalyst of Restoration

As the daughter of Henry VIII and his first wife, Catherine of Aragon, Mary inherited a realm fractured by the legacy of the English Reformation. Amidst this turmoil, she embarked on a mission to restore Roman Catholicism, unleashing a torrent of change that would forever reshape the course of English history.

Mary I's ascension to the throne was a pivotal moment in a nation torn asunder by the religious upheavals of her father's reign. Henry VIII's break with the Catholic Church had precipitated a seismic shift, with the dissolution of monasteries, the establishment of the Church of England, and the introduction of Protestant reforms.

Upon Edward's untimely death, the path was paved for Mary's accession, and with it, the promise of a return to the Catholic faith. This promise resonated deeply with Mary, a devout Catholic who had endured years of persecution and exile for her unwavering beliefs. As she ascended the throne, the nation held its breath, anticipating the profound changes that her reign would usher in.

Mary I faced a daunting task: to reverse the tides of Protestant reform that had swept across England during her father's and brother's reigns. The challenge was not merely one of religious doctrine but also of political and social upheaval. The Protestant faith had taken root, and its adherents held positions of power and influence across the realm.

Undeterred, Mary embarked on a series of bold measures to restore Catholic supremacy. She swiftly repealed the religious legislation of her predecessors, attempting to nullify the English Reformation and reinstate the authority of the Pope. The Mass was restored, and Catholic rituals and practices once again became the norm.

However, Mary's zeal for the Catholic cause extended far beyond mere policy changes. She saw herself as an instrument of divine providence, tasked with purging England of what she perceived as the heresy of Protestantism. This conviction gave rise to a period of intense persecution, as hundreds of Protestants were imprisoned, exiled, and in many cases, burned at the stake for their refusal to renounce their faith.

Mary I's unwavering commitment to the Catholic cause has often been oversimplified and distorted, casting her as a tyrannical and bloodthirsty ruler driven by religious fanaticism. This portrayal, while not entirely unfounded, fails to capture the nuances of her motivations and the complexities of the era in which she lived.

Typical approaches to understanding Mary's actions have often focused solely on the brutality of her persecutions, painting a one-dimensional picture of a monarch consumed by religious fervor. However, this narrow perspective overlooks the intricate web of political, social, and personal factors that shaped her reign.

Many have argued that Mary's reliance on force and coercion to impose religious conformity was misguided and ultimately counterproductive. The martyrdom of Protestants like Thomas Cranmer and Hugh Latimer only served to galvanize opposition and turn public sentiment against the Catholic cause. Yet, this assessment fails to acknowledge the cultural and religious climate of the time, where religious unity was seen as a cornerstone of national stability and the use of force was a common tool of governance.

To truly understand Mary I's determination to restore Roman Catholicism, a more nuanced approach is required – one that weaves together the threads of faith, politics, and personal conviction. By examining her actions through the lens of her upbringing, her experiences of persecution, and the tumultuous religious landscape she inherited, a richer narrative emerges.

Mary's steadfast adherence to Catholicism was not merely a matter of doctrine but a deeply personal belief forged in the crucible of adversity. As the daughter of Catherine of Aragon, she had witnessed firsthand the anguish and humiliation her mother endured due to Henry VIII's desire for a male heir and his subsequent divorce. This trauma, coupled with her own struggles during the reigns of her father and brother, instilled in Mary a profound sense of duty to defend the Catholic faith and restore its primacy in England.

Moreover, Mary's actions must be understood within the context of the prevailing belief that religious unity was essential for political stability and national security. In an era when religious dissent was often equated with treason, her persecution of Protestants was not merely an expression of religious zeal but a calculated effort to consolidate her power and secure the loyalty of her subjects.

While Mary I's reign was brief, spanning a mere five years, its impact on the religious and political landscape of England was profound. Her unwavering commitment to the Catholic cause yielded tangible results, as the nation witnessed a resurgence of Catholic practices, the restoration of monastic lands, and the reinstatement of Catholic bishops and clergy.

Ironically, however, the very force with which Mary pursued her religious agenda sowed the seeds of its eventual undoing. The executions of prominent Protestants like Thomas Cranmer only served to rally opposition and galvanize support for the Protestant cause. The persecutions were met with resistance, both overt and covert, as underground Protestant movements emerged, spreading English translations of the Bible and fostering a spirit of defiance.

Moreover, Mary's marriage to Philip II of Spain, a staunch Catholic, further fueled concerns about foreign influence and the erosion of English autonomy. This perception of Catholic encroachment on English sovereignty would ultimately contribute to the resurgence of Protestant sentiments under the reign of her successor, Elizabeth I.

Critics may argue that Mary I's actions were misguided and ultimately counterproductive, citing the resurgence of Protestantism under Elizabeth I and the enduring legacy of the English Reformation. They may question the wisdom of employing force to impose religious conformity, asserting that such measures only breed resentment and solidify resistance.

Ultimately, Mary I's determination to restore Roman Catholicism transcended religious doctrine or political calculation. It was a deeply personal crusade, driven by a conviction forged in the fires of adversity and a belief that she was an instrument of divine providence. Her actions, while controversial and often brutal, were a reflection of the profound power of faith and its ability to shape the course of nations and individuals alike.

As we reflect on the catalytic role Mary I played in the religious and political upheavals of Tudor England, we are reminded of the enduring relevance of faith and its ability to shape the course of human events. Her unwavering commitment to the Catholic cause, while often criticized, serves as a testament to the power of conviction and the lengths to which individuals will go to uphold their beliefs.

Rather than dismissing Mary's actions as the misguided efforts of a fanatic, we must understand the complexities of her motivations and the nuances of the historical context in which she lived. By doing so, we can gain a deeper appreciation for the intricate interplay between faith, politics, and personal conviction that defined her reign.

Moreover, Mary's legacy serves as a poignant reminder of the enduring impact of religious conviction on the course of history. Her persecutions, while brutal, ultimately sowed the seeds of Protestant resistance and paved the way for the religious settlements that would follow under Elizabeth I.

Defining the Marian Reformation

Delving into the intricacies of Mary I's religious policies and the tumultuous era of the English Reformation requires a firm grasp of key terms and concepts. Understanding the nuances of these pivotal ideas is crucial to appreciating the depth and significance of the events that unfolded during her reign. In the ensuing discourse, we shall illuminate these pivotal notions, paving the way for a comprehensive exploration of Mary's consequential actions.

The Marian Persecutions: A chilling phrase that conjures images of religious intolerance and brutality where almost three hundred people were executed. Yet, what were these persecutions, and what drove Mary to such extreme measures? Far from a mere exercise in cruelty, these persecutions were an embodiment of Mary's unwavering commitment to her faith and her determination to eradicate what she perceived as heresy from her realm.

Heretic: A term that has echoed throughout history, often accompanied by the crackling of flames and the cries of the condemned. In the context of Mary's reign, a heretic was anyone who dared to deviate from the Catholic doctrine, embracing the tenets of the Protestant Reformation.

Counter-Reformation: A sweeping movement that sought to combat the spread of Protestantism and reassert the authority of the Catholic Church. Mary's efforts to restore Catholicism in England were a pivotal part of this broader Counter-Reformation.

The Mass: At the heart of Catholic worship lies the Mass, a sacred ritual that commemorates the Last Supper and the sacrifice of Christ. When Mary ascended the throne, she swiftly reinstated the Latin Mass, reversing the reforms of her Protestant predecessors and restoring the traditional language and rituals that had defined English Catholicism for generations.

Iconoclasm: A term that encapsulates the destruction of religious imagery, an act that was embraced by Protestant reformers seeking to purge churches of what they deemed idolatrous representations. Mary's efforts to restore Catholic traditions involved the reversal of iconoclastic policies, ushering in the return of ornate statues, paintings, and other religious artworks to places of worship.

Ecclesiastical Hierarchy: The intricate structure of authority and governance within the Catholic Church, with the Pope at its apex. Mary's restoration of Catholicism necessitated the reinstatement of this hierarchy, including the reappointment of bishops and clergy who had been deposed during the Protestant reforms of her brother's reign.

The Marian Persecutions: A Crucible of Faith and Intolerance

At the heart of Mary's efforts to restore Catholicism lay the Marian Persecutions, a series of brutal acts that cast a long and ominous shadow over her reign. To Mary, these persecutions were not mere acts of cruelty but rather a necessary purge, a means of eradicating the scourge of heresy that had taken root in her kingdom.

The term "heretic" had long been a potent weapon in the arsenal of religious authorities, a label that could condemn individuals to exile, torture, or even execution. In the eyes of Mary and her Catholic advisors, the Protestant reformers who had gained influence during the reigns of her father and brother were not merely misguided souls; they were dangerous heretics, threatening to unravel the very fabric of English society and imperil the souls of her subjects.

The persecutions themselves were a grim spectacle, with prominent Protestant leaders such as Thomas Cranmer, the Archbishop of Canterbury, and Hugh Latimer, the Bishop of Worcester, condemned to the flames. The sight of these once-revered figures being burned at the stake sent shockwaves through the nation, stoking fears of a return to the darkest days of religious intolerance.

Yet, to Mary, these acts were not merely a means of silencing dissent; they were a sacred duty, a necessary sacrifice to preserve the purity of the Catholic faith and safeguard the spiritual wellbeing of her subjects. In her mind, the heretics were not merely challenging her authority as monarch but also defying the immutable truths of the Church, a transgression that could not be tolerated.

Timeline of Restoration and Conflict

Mary I's reign witnessed a pivotal chapter in the religious and political history of England, as she embarked on an uncompromising campaign to restore Roman Catholicism as the nation's preeminent faith. This timeline chronicles the key events that marked her efforts to repudiate the Protestant Reformation and reaffirm the authority of the Church of Rome, while also illustrating how these religious policies intertwined with her military engagements and international alliances.

By understanding the religious fervor, political maneuvering, and military conflict, we can better appreciate the enduring impact of Mary's reign on the English nation's spiritual and temporal trajectories.

While the seeds of the English Reformation can be traced back to the early 16th century, with figures like John Wycliffe and the Lollard movement challenging the Catholic Church's dominance, Mary I's zeal for restoring the Roman faith stemmed from her fervent Catholic upbringing and her unwavering allegiance to her mother, Catherine of Aragon.

From her earliest years, Mary was indoctrinated in the tenets of Catholicism, imbued with a deep reverence for the Church's traditions and a profound distrust of the Protestant heresies that had begun to take root in England.

Key Events: Restoring Catholic Supremacy and Engaging in Conflict

- 1553: Mary I ascends to the throne after the brief reign of her Protestant half-brother, Edward VI. She immediately begins laying the groundwork for the restoration of Catholicism, seeking reconciliation with the Papacy and petitioning for absolution from the schism initiated by her father, Henry VIII.

- 1554: The Act of Supremacy, which had established Henry VIII as the head of the Church of England, is revoked, and England is officially reconciled with the Roman Catholic Church. The Latin Mass and Catholic rituals are reinstated, while Protestant practices are outlawed.

- 1555: The Court of High Commission, a powerful inquisitorial body, is established to investigate and prosecute those deemed to be heretics or non-conformists. This marks the beginning of a brutal campaign of persecution against Protestants, with hundreds being interrogated, tortured, and, in many cases, executed for their refusal to renounce their faith.

- 1555-1556: The executions of Thomas Cranmer (former Archbishop of Canterbury), Nicholas Ridley (Bishop of

London), and Hugh Latimer (renowned Church of England cleric) take place in Oxford, serving as a chilling reminder of Mary's unwavering resolve and the grave consequences that awaited those who defied her Catholic edicts.

- 1557: Mary I marries Philip II of Spain, solidifying an alliance with the powerful Catholic monarchy and further strengthening her resolve to eradicate Protestantism from England. This unpopular marriage, however, sows the seeds of resentment and unrest among her subjects.

- 1557-1558: Embroiled in a conflict with France, known as the Anglo-French War (1557-1559), Mary I allies with her husband, Philip II of Spain, in a military campaign against the French. This war, driven by religious and territorial disputes, sees England and Spain battling French forces in regions such as Calais and Saint-Quentin.

- 1558: As her reign draws to a close, Mary I's legacy is one of both triumph and turmoil. She has succeeded in reversing the tide of the English Reformation and restoring the Catholic Church's authority, but at the cost of widespread persecution and an unpopular foreign alliance that has bred discontent among her subjects.

Adaptations and Regional Differences

While Mary I's efforts to restore Catholicism were focused primarily on England, her reign also had ripple effects throughout the British Isles and beyond. In Ireland, for instance, the Catholic faith remained deeply entrenched, and Mary's policies were largely welcomed, further solidifying the island's allegiance to Rome.

In Scotland, however, the Protestant Reformation had gained a stronger foothold, with figures like John Knox leading the charge against Catholic doctrine and practices. Mary's religious policies were met with resistance and stoked tensions between the two nations.

Contemporary Relevance and Legacy

The legacy of Mary I's reign and her efforts to restore Catholicism continue to resonate in modern times. Her zeal for religious orthodoxy and her willingness to employ brutal measures to suppress dissent have been the subject of ongoing historical analysis and debate.

Moreover, the enduring tensions between Catholic and Protestant factions, particularly in regions like Northern Ireland, can be traced back, in part, to the religious upheavals of Mary's reign and the lasting impact of her policies on the spiritual and cultural fabric of the British Isles.

Pivotal Moments and Challenges

While Mary I's reign was marked by numerous victories in her campaign to restore Catholicism, it was not without significant challenges and pivotal moments that threatened to derail her efforts.

One such moment came in 1554, when the Wyatt Rebellion erupted, with Protestant rebels seeking to depose Mary and install her Protestant sister, Elizabeth, on the throne. Though the rebellion was ultimately quashed, it underscored the depth of resentment and opposition that Mary's religious policies had engendered among segments of the population.

Another pivotal challenge arose from within Mary's own court, as some of her advisors and councilors grew increasingly concerned about the severity of her persecutions and the potential for widespread unrest. These internal tensions and debates over the appropriate extent of religious suppression added further complexity to Mary's crusade and highlighted the delicate balance she sought to maintain between religious fervor and political pragmatism.

In the end, Mary I's unwavering commitment to restoring Catholicism defined her reign and left an indelible mark on the history of England and the broader British Isles. Her efforts, though ultimately reversed by her successor, Elizabeth I, remain a testament to the enduring power of religious conviction and the profound impact that faith can have on the course of nations.

Elizabeth I
Reign 1558-1603

Transition of Power

The transition from Mary I to Elizabeth I represents not merely a change in monarchs but a pivotal shift in the religious and political ethos of Tudor England. Elizabeth's ascension to the throne in 1558 was met with a kingdom deeply divided by religious strife and the lingering scars of her sister's persecutions. Yet, it was under Elizabeth's reign that England would witness a period of relative stability, cultural renaissance, and the strengthening of the Protestant faith, all of which were navigated with a shrewdness that was emblematic of her rule.

1558-1603: Elizabeth I's era, often heralded as the Elizabethan Age, marks a golden epoch in English history, characterized by diplomatic finesse, the flourishing of the arts, and the consolidation of Protestantism. Her approach to the religious divide, encapsulated in the Elizabethan Religious Settlement of 1559, sought to establish a middle ground between the extremes of Catholicism and Protestantism. This pragmatic stance, while not without its critics, laid the foundations for the Church of England and endeavored to unite her subjects under a common religious framework.

Elizabeth's foreign policy was equally notable, balancing the intricate dance of diplomacy with major European powers such as Spain and France. Her ability to maintain peace through strategic alliances, coupled with a keen sense of when to engage in or avoid conflict, allowed England to navigate the treacherous waters of international politics with remarkable success. The defeat of the Spanish Armada in 1588, often seen as Elizabeth's crowning achievement, not only secured England's independence from Spanish ambitions but also established it as a formidable naval power.

Culturally, Elizabeth's reign was a renaissance of its own, nurturing the talents of playwrights, poets, and musicians. The patronage of figures like William Shakespeare, Christopher Marlowe, and Thomas Tallis contributed to an unprecedented flourishing of English arts and literature, reflecting the vibrancy and dynamism of the Elizabethan court.

However, Elizabeth's policies and the stability of her reign were not without their challenges. The question of succession loomed large, with Elizabeth's refusal to marry or name an heir causing unease among her council and subjects. Moreover, the religious settlement, while successful in quelling the immediate divisions, did not entirely extinguish the flames of dissent, with periodic challenges from both Catholic and Puritan factions.

Elizabeth's governance also saw England's initial forays into colonial expansion and the slave trade, ventures that would have lasting implications for English and global history. Her support for explorers like Sir Walter Raleigh and Sir Francis Drake laid the groundwork for the British Empire, yet also entangled England in the moral and ethical complexities of colonialism and exploitation.

In the Shadow of Mary Tudor

In juxtaposing Elizabeth's formative years with those of her half-sister, Mary I, we unearth layers of familial and political intrigue that prefigured the labyrinthine dynamics of Tudor succession.

Mary's early life, steeped in the Catholic tradition and the favor of their father, Henry VIII, before his break with the Church of Rome, contrasts sharply with Elizabeth's upbringing in the nascent Church of England, a church whose very establishment rendered Elizabeth's mother, Anne Boleyn, and consequently Elizabeth herself, as contentious figures in the eyes of Catholics both in England and abroad.

The purpose of this comparison is not merely to delineate two divergent paths within the same royal lineage but to illuminate how these early experiences forged two distinct worldviews, ultimately influencing their respective reigns.

By examining the nuances of their upbringings, religious orientations, and early political experiences, we can glean insights into Elizabeth's political acumen and her adeptness at navigating the treacherous waters of religious and political factionalism that defined her era.

One might ponder, for instance, how Elizabeth's perception of her Catholic sister's reign, marked by attempts at religious reversion and the infamous Marian persecutions, where 300 protestants were executed as heretics, informed her own policy of religious tolerance.

Did the specter of her sister's efforts to restore Catholicism, which led to widespread unrest and earned Mary the epithet 'Bloody Mary,' serve as a cautionary tale for Elizabeth, thereby shaping her more measured approach to religious policy?

The similarities in their circumstances, both daughters of Henry VIII striving to assert their legitimacy and authority in a male-dominated society and a tumultuous political landscape, underscore the resilience and determination that characterized their reigns.

Yet, their divergent responses to the challenges they faced reveal much about their individual characters and the distinct strategies they employed to consolidate their power.

Elizabeth's strategy of religious tolerance, compared to Mary's staunch Catholicism, not only reflects their personal convictions but also their political sagacity.

Elizabeth's approach fostered a more stable and prosperous England, free from the religious strife that marred her sister's reign.

This difference in approach speaks volumes about Elizabeth's understanding of the delicate balance required to govern a divided nation, a skill seemingly honed from observing the pitfalls that beset her half-sister's rule.

Moreover, Elizabeth's decision to remain unmarried, thereby retaining complete control over her political and bodily autonomy, contrasts markedly with Mary's marriage to Philip II of Spain.

This union, while politically motivated, failed to secure the Catholic succession Mary so desperately sought and further alienated her from her subjects.

Elizabeth's observation of Mary's marital alliance, and its repercussions, may well have influenced her own decision to eschew marriage, viewing it as a potential encumbrance to her sovereignty and to England's independence.

These reflections on the parallels and divergences in the lives of Elizabeth and Mary I open a window into the complex interplay of personal beliefs, political necessity, and historical context.

The contrast between Elizabeth's judicious exercise of power and Mary's more doctrinaire approach offers a profound commentary on the nature of leadership and the eternal quest for a balance between conviction and compromise.

In delving into the implications of their relationship and contrasting reigns, we uncover not just the personal rivalry that history often highlights, but a deeper narrative about the evolution of governance, the role of women in power, and the transformative impact of religious belief on statecraft.

Elizabeth's ability to learn from her sister's experiences, adapting and refining her strategies, showcases a level of political finesse and foresight that not only distinguished her reign but also redefined the monarchy for generations to come.

Thus, as we trace the arc of Elizabeth's ascendancy against the backdrop of her familial dynamics, particularly her relationship with Mary, we gain a more nuanced understanding of the forces that shaped not only a queen but an era.

The interplay between their shared heritage and their divergent paths to power illuminates the complexities of Tudor politics, the fraught nature of succession, and the indelible impact of these two formidable women on the course of English history.

Navigating Royal Hostility

With the intricate interlacing of Elizabeth and Mary's narratives setting the stage, it becomes incumbent upon us to delve deeper into the crucible of conflict and conciliation that defined Elizabeth's ascent to power. This exploration necessitates a foray into the realm of espionage and intelligence, a domain where shadows danced with light, and the pen proved mightier than the sword.

The establishment of the first state-sponsored secret service under the guidance of Sir Francis Walsingham, Elizabeth's spymaster, marked a seminal moment in the annals of intelligence operations, underscoring the queen's adeptness at wielding information as both shield and spear against internal dissent and external threats.

Walsingham's network of spies, informants, and codebreakers stretched across Europe, turning the continent into a chessboard where moves were anticipated and countered with meticulous precision. This web of espionage was not merely a tool for safeguarding the realm but a manifestation of Elizabeth's recognition of the power of information.

In an era where the flow of knowledge was as tightly controlled as the borders of nations, Elizabeth's investment in intelligence gathering highlighted her strategic foresight and her understanding of its significance in the broader geopolitical landscape.

Consider, for instance, the Throckmorton Plot and the Babington Plot, both of which sought to place Mary Queen of Scots on the English throne and restore Catholicism. Through Walsingham's diligent efforts, these conspiracies were unearthed and thwarted, thereby not only preserving Elizabeth's reign but also demonstrating the efficacy of espionage in the maintenance of sovereign security.

These incidents, while reinforcing Elizabeth's authority, also illuminate her governance style, one characterized by pragmatism, adaptability, and an unyielding resolve to protect her kingdom.

Yet, the employment of espionage raises ethical questions that merit contemplation. In the pursuit of security, where does one draw the line between vigilance and violation? Elizabeth's era, much like our own, grappled with the balance between privacy and protection, a dilemma that remains as pertinent today as it was in the 16th century.

The queen's reliance on intelligence operations, while undeniably effective, also invites us to reflect on the moral imperatives of leadership and the costs associated with the preservation of power.

Furthermore, Elizabeth's engagement with the arts and culture offers yet another vantage point from which to appreciate her multidimensional approach to governance. The patronage of playwrights, poets, and artists under her reign catalyzed a cultural renaissance that not only beautified her court but also served as a soft power strategy, enhancing England's prestige abroad and fostering national pride at home.

The flourishing of the Elizabethan theatre, epitomized by the works of William Shakespeare, and the advancements in literature, science, and exploration during this period, were not mere coincidences but the fruit of a deliberate policy to elevate the cultural standing of the kingdom.

This cultural efflorescence, juxtaposed with the grim undertones of espionage, paints a portrait of Elizabeth as a ruler who navigated the complexities of her role with an astute understanding of the multifaceted nature of power.

She recognized that the strength of her reign lay not only in the might of her navy or the depth of her coffers but in the richness of her kingdom's cultural life and the loyalty of her subjects, nurtured through both spectacle and surveillance.

As we venture further into the labyrinth of Elizabeth's political and personal odyssey, it becomes evident that her legacy is a palimpsest of triumphs and tribulations, of visible achievements and shadowy machinations.

Her reign, a confluence of art and espionage, of public display and private intelligence, challenges us to ponder the dualities inherent in governance and the enduring quest for a legacy that transcends the vicissitudes of time and the judgment of history.

In examining the tapestry of Elizabeth's reign, we are reminded of the enduring interplay between power and perception, between the image a monarch projects and the reality of their rule.

Elizabeth's ability to cultivate an image of invincibility and wisdom, to command the loyalty of her subjects through a combination of fear, admiration, and love, underscores the performative aspects of monarchy.

It invites us to consider the ways in which leaders, past and present, use symbolism, ritual, and spectacle to reinforce their authority and inscribe their rule in the collective memory of their people.

Thus, as we dissect the layers of Elizabeth's governance, her strategies for survival, and her quest for immortality through cultural patronage and statecraft, we are drawn into a deeper contemplation of the essence of leadership.

The narrative of Elizabeth I, fraught with peril and punctuated by moments of unparalleled brilliance, offers a mirror into the soul of power itself, reflecting the perennial challenges of steering the ship of state through the uncharted waters of political tumult and societal change.

The Making of a Queen

In the intricate dance of power and perception that defined Elizabeth I's reign, the interplay between personal liberty and public responsibility emerges as a central theme. This dynamic, while not unique to Elizabeth's era, took on particular significance in the context of her leadership, illuminating the ways in which the personal and the political were inextricably linked in the life of a monarch.

Elizabeth's personal beliefs and desires, often subsumed beneath the weight of her royal duties, provide a poignant lens through which to view the sacrifices inherent in her position. Her choice to remain unmarried, for example, while politically astute, also reflected a deeper negotiation between her private inclinations and the public good. This decision, often celebrated as a masterstroke of political strategy, also hints at the personal cost of such a choice, raising questions about the intersection of duty and desire in the life of a leader.

Moreover, Elizabeth's relationships with her advisors and courtiers offer a window into the complexities of royal intimacy. The trust she placed in figures like Sir Francis Walsingham and Robert Dudley was not merely a matter of political convenience but a reflection of her human need for connection and counsel. Yet, these relationships were also fraught with political implications, demonstrating the delicate balance Elizabeth had to maintain between personal loyalty and the imperatives of statecraft.

The cultivation of her public image, a blend of majesty and relatability, further underscores the performative aspects of her reign. Elizabeth's adept use of symbolism, from the choice of attire to the staging of public appearances, was not simply an exercise in vanity but a strategic tool for reinforcing her authority and engendering a sense of national unity. This conscious construction of her persona, while effective in consolidating her power, also invites reflection on the role of authenticity and representation in leadership.

Elizabeth's patronage of the arts, while a testament to her appreciation for culture and intellect, also served a political purpose, embedding her legacy within the cultural fabric of the nation. The promotion of the Elizabethan theatre and the arts was not only a means of celebrating English talent but also a way of shaping the narrative of her reign, crafting an image of prosperity and enlightenment that would endure beyond her lifetime. This strategic engagement with culture highlights the intersection of aesthetics and power, suggesting that the legacy of a leader is not only written in the annals of history but also inscribed in the cultural memory of their time.

The challenges Elizabeth faced, from domestic unrest to foreign threats, required not just political acumen but a profound resilience. Her ability to navigate these challenges, to turn potential weaknesses into strengths, speaks to a deeper understanding of the human spirit and the art of governance. The Armada portrait, commemorating the defeat of the Spanish Armada, serves as a symbol of this resilience, portraying Elizabeth not just as a monarch but as a manifestation of national pride and determination.

In delving into the layers of Elizabeth's reign, we observe not only the mechanics of power but also the human dimensions of leadership. The balance between the public persona and the private individual, between the performative and the authentic, offers a nuanced perspective on the burdens and the privileges of rule. Elizabeth's story, with its blend of triumph and tribulation, invites us to consider the enduring question of what it means to lead, to weigh the needs of the many against the desires of the few, and to craft a legacy that withstands the test of time.

As we consider the final chapters of Elizabeth's life and the transition of power to James I, we are reminded of the cyclical nature of history and the fleetingness of power. The end of the Elizabethan era, while marking the close of a significant chapter in English history, also signals the beginning of a new narrative, one that would build upon and diverge from the foundations laid by Elizabeth. This transition, fraught with its own set of challenges and opportunities, underscores the continuity of governance and the evolving nature of leadership.

The legacy of Elizabeth I, complex and multifaceted, continues to captivate and inspire. It compels us to reflect on the intersections of history and humanity, of power and perception, inviting us to ponder the myriad ways in which leaders shape and are shaped by their times. In the final analysis, Elizabeth's reign serves as a testament to the enduring impact of visionary leadership and the indelible mark it leaves on the fabric of history.

The End of the Tudor Dynasty

The death of Elizabeth I in 1603, marking the end of the Tudor dynasty, heralded the beginning of the Stuart era. Her legacy, a complex amalgam of triumph, tragedy, and transformation, left an indelible mark on the nation's consciousness. The Elizabethan Age, with its achievements in governance, culture, and exploration, stands as a testament to the power of leadership and vision in shaping the destiny of a nation. In reflecting on the reigns of Henry VII, Henry VIII, Edward VI, Mary I, and Elizabeth I, we are presented with a tableau of Tudor England in all its contrasts—its religious fervor and reforms, its political machinations, and its cultural renaissance. These monarchs, with their distinct approaches to rule, personify the tumult and triumphs of an era that was foundational to the shaping of modern England. Their stories, interwoven with the tapestry of Tudor history, highlight the enduring interplay between individual leadership, religion, and the collective destiny of a nation.

Don't miss out!

Visit the website below and you can sign up to receive emails whenever History Nerds publishes a new book. There's no charge and no obligation.

https://books2read.com/r/B-A-ODOK-CHCHD

BOOKS 2 READ

Connecting independent readers to independent writers.

Also by History Nerds

Ancient Empires
The Ottoman Empire
Rome: The Rise and Fall
The Mongol Empire
The Assyrian Empire
Ancient Egypt

Celtic Heroes and Legends
Celtic History
William Butler Yeats: Nobel Prize Winning Poet
Robert the Bruce
Scáthach
Finn McCool
William Wallace: Scotland's Great Freedom Fighter

Frauen des Krieges
Boudica: Königin der Icener
Jeanne d'Arc

Irena Sendler

Great Wars of the World
World War 1
World War 2
The Napoleonic Wars: One Shot at Glory
The Serbian Revolution: 1804-1835
Peace Won by the Saber: The Crimean War, 1853-1856
The American Civil War

Pirate Chronicles
Grace O'Malley: The Pirate Queen of Ireland
Blackbeard
William Kidd
Ching Shih
Anne Bonny

The History of England
Roman Britain
Medieval England
The Wars of the Roses
Tudor England

The History of the Vikings

Vikings
Longships on Restless Seas

Women of War
Boudica: Queen of the Iceni
Joan of Arc
Irena Sendler
Virginia Hall
Queen Amanirenas
Women of War Omnibus: Books 1-5

World History
The History of the United Kingdom
The History of Ireland
The History of America
The History of Scotland
The History of Wales
The History of India

Standalone
Grace O'Malley: Die Piratenkönigin von Irland

www.ingramcontent.com/pod-product-compliance
Lightning Source LLC
Chambersburg PA
CBHW021332160726
47994CB00007B/2654